CLAUDIA HENDERSON

MEMORIES

FROM

THE

ROAD

LESS

TRAVELED

(Devotional Book)

susannasheehy@yahoo.com

ISBN: 978-0-9789271-9-6

Elden Publishing, LLC

Illustrations by **Craig Henderson**

Endorsements

Ron and Claudia Henderson are two of God's choicest servants, and two of my favorite people. For forty-five years they have faithfully served the Lord in music evangelism with the utmost of integrity. As Georgia Baptists, we claim them as a vital part of our family, but their ministry has taken them across the country and into the hearts of all who have heard them. In this wonderful book, Claudia pulls back the curtain to allow the reader a look behind the scenes of their ministry. No doubt you will be deeply moved, will laugh, and perhaps shed a tear as you read these marvelous stories.

J. Robert White
Executive Director Emeritus
Georgia Baptist Mission Board
President and CEO
Georgia Baptist Health Care Ministry Foundation

Ron and Claudia Henderson are two of my very favorite friends and I am so excited about her new devotional book, **Memories From The Road Less Traveled.** As one who has traveled that same road for over fifty years, I too can identify with her wise and encouraging observations. It is a book to read, treasure and share!

Evangelist Junior Hill

I am excited about this new book of stories from the road by my friends and long-time Sherwood members, Ron and Claudia Henderson. Life on the road as traveling evangelists is difficult and, at times, impossible. Ron and Claudia have navigated decades of ministry and thousands of concerts as faithful road warriors. These stories will bless and inspire you, and some might even cause you to cringe. They're all true. This couple has stayed out of the ruts, overcome some potholes, avoided the detours, and taken the narrow road in a world where the wide road is far more appealing and "successful." Well done, my friends! Thank you for sharing your lives – and these stories – with the rest of us.

Michael Catt
Senior Pastor
Sherwood Baptist Church | Albany, Georgia

DEDICATION

This book is lovingly dedicated to my husband, Ron, with whom I've shared 49 precious years of marriage. Through his FAITH, I've been strengthened. Through his LAUGHTER, I've known joy. Through his WORDS, I've gained understanding, and through his SMILE, I've felt approval. His hand has guided me and his love has sustained me. He has been to me a reflection of the One who gives purpose to everything.

> Ron,
>
> For every day we've shared,
>
> For every song we've sung,
>
> For every mile we've walked,
>
> For every victory won...
>
> I thank God for your life,
>
> For love that you impart,
>
> And all the "precious memories"
>
> He's placed within my heart.
>
> I love you,
>
> Claudia

INTRODUCTION

It is my prayer that this book will be an encouragement to your heart, as you experience through our lives and ministry, the sweet grace extended to us by the outstretched hand of our Lord.

At the beginning of our journey, the "Road" that Ron and I traveled in Evangelism seemed vast and crowded. But as the years passed, there were fewer travelers on this road. Today, there are few who travel the road of the Vocational Evangelist.

In his poem, "The Road Not Taken," Robert Frost said:

"Two roads diverged in a wood, and I –

 I took the one less traveled by,

 And that has made all the difference."

Because we chose to follow wherever God led, He has made the difference in our lives. Thank you, Lord, for the treasured

"Memories From The Road Less Traveled".

Claudia Henderson

MEMORY 1

Ron and I were visiting his parents in Montgomery, Alabama. Their church was in revival during our visit, so we attended ALL of the services. R. L. and Beth Sigrest, music evangelists from Mississippi, were presenting the music for the meeting. As they sang, the Lord spoke to us through their beautiful music. It was a definite call to serve Him in a music ministry... but how? Ron was employed by a Georgia corporation and we were anxiously awaiting the birth of our son. Neither of us felt qualified in the field of music, but the tug at our hearts to follow the Lord's will became even stronger.

Two months after the revival with the Sigrests the Lord gave us a precious son, Craig. We were so excited with the abundance of blessings in our lives... a new baby, a good job, a wonderful church family, and a bright future in Albany. But the Lord still spoke about His music... His joy... His peace... and we began to realize as we lived our "normal" lives, that we weren't truly happy. We had chosen frustration and discontent over obedience!

After two years of inner turmoil, Ron resigned his job and we stepped out on faith to serve the Lord through music. This step of faith was possible because of the people whom the Lord placed in our lives to strengthen and nurture us. One such friend was Ted Moody.

Ted was in evangelism, and preaching a revival in Albany when we met him. We had been invited to sing a couple of songs at that meeting, and afterward, we talked to Ted about our desire to enter the field of music evangelism. Ted said he could use us in two meetings that year, and it was at this point that Ron severed his ties with the company that employed him

With our small son, our compact car, no guaranteed income, no sound equipment, and no experience, we began a walk of faith and obedience.

As you read Isaiah 55: 8-12, be assured that your obedient response to His voice will bring lasting peace and joy to your life.

Isaiah 55

8 For my thoughts are not your thoughts, neither are your ways my ways, saith the Lord.

9 For as the heavens are higher than the earth, so are my ways higher than your ways, and my thoughts than your thoughts.

10 For as the rain cometh down, and the snow from heaven, and returneth not thither, but watereth the earth, and maketh it bring forth and bud, that it may give seed to the sower, and bread to the eater:

11 So shall my word be that goeth forth out of my mouth: it shall not return unto me void, but it shall accomplish that which I please, and it shall prosper in the thing whereto I sent it.

12 For ye shall go out with joy, and be led forth with peace...

MEMORY 2

When we are obedient to the voice of the Lord, there is a calm in our spirit and a peace that passes all understanding. Even though we were uncertain as to where the Lord would lead us, we were confident from that first step of faith that He would be faithful in His call.

How does God go about confirming His call in our lives? By following His will, we were placed in some very unique circumstances... circumstances that differed from our normal lifestyle... circumstances which involved our total dependence upon God.

We had a desire to serve the Lord through music... and though we lacked confidence in our ability, we made ourselves available to Him by accepting an invitation to do the music for a revival in Ashburn, Georgia. Ron was still employed with a local business at the time, and we were excited about getting to sing every night for an entire week. The Lord sent one of His choice servants, Cecil Clegg, to preach the meeting in Ashburn. As Cecil preached each night, the Lord spoke to us and confirmed our decision to walk by faith and not by sight.

Yes, we ate Rolaids and drank Pepto Bismol. And yes, our knees shook each time we stood before a congregation. In fact, when the Lord called us, we were a whole lot like Moses when the Lord called him...

> *I used to be like Moses when he said,*
>   *"Lord, I can't speak."*
> *My stomach hurt so very bad.*
>   *My body was so weak.*
> *I thought I had a nervous twitch,*
>   *My knees were knocking, too.*
> *I said, "Dear Lord, you can't use me!*

There's someone better who
Can sing Your praises, share Your love,
Tell others what You've done.
I'm sure there must be someone else.
I know I'm not the one."

And then my thoughts went drifting back
To Calvary, where He died.
I saw Him there upon that tree,
And lost my foolish pride.
I heard Him say from Calvary,
"I'm doing this for you."
I bowed my head and to Him said,
"I'll go, I'll sing, I'll do
Whatever You might ask of me.
My life I give to You."

(poem by Claudia Henderson)

As you read Isaiah 6: 8, remember that He said **yes** to the cross. How can you say **no** to Him?

Isaiah 6

8 Also I heard the voice of the Lord, saying, "Whom shall I send, and who will go for us?" Then said I, "Here am I! Send me."

MEMORY 3

We always remember the "firsts" in our lives... and our "first" revival in full time evangelism was truly a memorable experience. We had no means of support and no way to provide our own lodging. We were dependent upon the churches we served for our financial needs.

Our lodging for our first revival was in a pastor's home. Ron, Craig, and I occupied an upstairs bedroom. Craig slept on the floor all week, and the bathroom was shared with the pastor's three children. There was little privacy, but a very special love surrounded us in that home.

At the end of the week-long revival, we were given our "first" paycheck in evangelism... $100. It wouldn't buy a sound system, a travel trailer for lodging, or a new van to pull the trailer... but it affirmed God's promise of faithfulness in the lives of His children, and we anxiously awaited our next engagement.

Our "first" year on the road made us appreciate all of the blessings we would receive as our ministry continued. We learned what it meant to be totally dependent upon God to supply our needs. Our "first" December in evangelism was one of those lean months. Our entire income for December was the $50 we received for a concert – our only engagement that month. Our families sustained us during these times, and we reciprocated with the completion of odd jobs such as painting their houses, cutting their grass, etc.

We finished that "first" year with 17 revivals. The Lord was so gracious to meet our needs, and with each touch of His hand upon our lives, we loved Him more!

As you read Psalm 139: 1-10, thank God for the guidance and love of His strong hand.

Psalm 139

1 O Lord, thou hast searched me, and known me.

2 Thou knowest my downsitting and mine uprising, thou understandest my thought afar off.

3 Thou compassest my path and my lying down, and art acquainted with all my ways.

4 For there is not a word in my tongue, but, lo, O Lord, thou knowest it altogether.

5 Thou hast beset me behind and before, and laid thine hand upon me.

6 Such knowledge is too wonderful for me; it is high, I cannot attain unto it.

7 Whither shall I go from thy spirit? or whither shall I flee from thy presence?

8 If I ascend up into heaven, thou art there: if I make my bed in hell, behold, thou art there.

9 If I take the wings of the morning, and dwell in the uttermost parts of the sea;

10 Even there shall thy hand lead me, and thy right hand shall hold me.

MEMORY 4

We did not purchase our first travel trailer (for lodging during revivals) until the end of our second year in evangelism. We continued to stay in motels and homes, as the churches provided. Many of the churches were small, and the cost of a motel room for our family's lodging was not an option. Thus, we were part of a different family unit each week.

Having so many different "homes" was difficult in some respects. No two families were alike. So, each week, we adjusted to a new family – their food, their houses, their habits, etc. We really had no private time for the three of us. In some of the homes, family members smoked, and we fought sinus problems, sore throats, and fumes during our stay.

Living out of a suitcase for two years had its unique moments. Sometimes we washed our clothes at a laund-ro-mat. At times, we were invited to use the washer and dryer at the home where we were staying. At other times, our hostess volunteered to do our laundry. I always preferred to wash our own "dirty" laundry... but on one occasion, this was not possible. Let me explain.

Ron, Craig, and I were guests in a home located in an historic area. We left the house early one morning to go sight-seeing... spent several hours enjoying historical places. When we returned to the house, we noticed that the laundry had been washed and was drying all along the banister of the stairway. A closer look at the laundry revealed a strange familiarity. These were our clothes that had been laundered in our absence! Since the dryer had broken down, our clothes (underwear and all!) were drying in various places throughout the house.

As we look back on this experience and similar ones, we realize that God was teaching us something about contentment. It's often difficult to accept the circumstances of our existence, but His grace is always sufficient for our need.

As you read I Timothy 6: 6-8, thank God for contentment that only He can give, as you place yourself in submission to Him.

I Timothy 6

6 Now godliness with contentment is great gain.

7 For we brought nothing into this world, and it is certain we can carry nothing out.

8 And having food and clothing, with these we shall be content.

Do you ever wonder how much of your teaching is retained by your children? Do they remember those important things you said... those things that can help them overcome difficult situations?

We were in revival at McRae, Georgia, staying at a local motel. The motel had a large swimming pool, and one hot afternoon, we decided to enjoy the water. Our son, Craig, was four years old... and to him, this pool was as vast as an ocean. He had been playing in the shallow end of the pool for some time, but gradually drifted to deeper water. When Craig realized he was no longer able to touch the bottom of the pool, he stretched his hands out over the water and cried, "Peace be still, I told you! Peace be still!" Craig was applying what he had learned from a familiar Bible story as an answer to a frantic situation.

As you read Philippians 4: 6-7, thank God for His peace in the midst of the storms you face, and ask Him for wisdom to appropriate the peace which passes our understanding.

Philippians 4

6 Be careful for nothing; but in every thing by prayer and supplication with thanksgiving let your requests be made known unto God.

7 And the peace of God, which passeth all understanding, shall keep your hearts and minds through Christ Jesus.

We were unable to purchase a travel trailer until the end of our second year in evangelism. It had been our dream to provide our own lodging during revivals, and in 1977, that dream became a reality. We bought a 29-foot trailer for $6,000. Even though our location changed from week to week, we had our home with us wherever we went. This was especially important for our 4 year old Craig, because now he was able to take his toys with him, and he even had a special place to keep everything!

Pulling the new trailer from place to place was sometimes difficult, depending on the weather. Our 1977 Caprice was not the best vehicle for pulling the trailer, but Ron managed it beautifully. We had only one mishap, and that occurred on a rainy Saturday as we were traveling to Alabama for a concert. When the car in front of us stopped to pick up a hitchhiker, it didn't pull off the road. With the weight of the travel trailer behind us, and the slick wet pavement beneath us, we plowed into the back of the car. No one was hurt, but the car that we hit was totaled. The driver of the car was so drunk he hardly knew what hit him!

There was little damage to our car (none to the trailer). God had been so good to protect us – and so merciful to give the drunk driver another day to straighten out his life.

As you read Psalm 91: 1, 2, and 11, thank Him for His care and protection, as well as His redemptive power to change lives.

Psalm 91

1 He that dwelleth in the secret place of the most High shall abide under the shadow of the Almighty.

2 I will say of the LORD, He is my refuge and my fortress: my God; in him will I trust.

11 For he shall give his angels charge over thee, to keep thee in all thy ways.

MEMORY 7

We will always remember our first revival in Kentucky. It was an old-fashioned tent meeting! Up to this time, we had sung in churches, and had no idea what to expect "under the big blue tent."

It had rained a lot the week before the Kentucky meeting, and the grass inside the tent was knee-deep! The rain was also responsible for a bumper crop of grasshoppers. Each night before the people arrived at the meeting, Ron, Craig, and I would roll up Craig's color books and use them to swat grasshoppers inside the tent. We fought a losing battle. During the services, the grasshoppers leaped from person to person amid giggles, gasps, and gulps.

In addition to the rain and grasshoppers, we faced a small medical crisis. Craig was playing on his skateboard in the parking lot adjacent to the tent when he fell and burst open his chin. We hurried to the hospital emergency room where the injury required stitches. I can still remember hearing Craig scream for us as we waited outside the emergency room. We were young, in strange surroundings, very little money and no means with which to pay the medical bills.

In situations such as this, we learned to wait on the Lord. He has always met our needs, and this was no exception. One of the churches sponsoring the tent crusade paid our hospital bill, and the Lord blessed in a multitude of ways during our stay in Kentucky.

As you read Isaiah 40: 28-31, thank God for His strength to meet your need as you wait patiently on Him today.

28 Hast thou not known? hast thou not heard, that the everlasting God, the Lord, the Creator of the ends of the earth, fainteth not, neither is weary? there is no searching of his understanding.

29 He giveth power to the faint; and to them that have no might he increaseth strength.

30 Even the youths shall faint and be weary, and the young men shall utterly fall:

31 But they that wait upon the Lord shall renew their strength; they shall mount up with wings as eagles; they shall run, and not be weary; and they shall walk, and not faint.

MEMORY 8

It was the morning of Lorraine's cancer surgery. She was a young mother who had a secretarial job with the State Health Department of Alabama. Doctors had recently found cancerous tissue in one of her hands. Today's surgery could mean the loss of her hand, her job, and the ability to function in her normal manner.

I awoke early on this day and began to pray for Lorraine. My mind was filled with thoughts of what she must be experiencing, especially the emotional trauma. Would the Lord heal her? I prayed that He would, if it were His will... and I prayed that she might have an overwhelming sense of His presence, that His peace which passes all understanding would keep her heart and mind on Him. As I prayed for Lorraine, the Lord put a song of assurance in my heart, and I wrote "My Precious Friend" for her.

My precious friend, as you wait on the Lord
Be assured that He's already there.
He's listening, and caring, and loving you so
He hears your heart's humble prayer.

My precious friend, He is longing to give
A peace, and a calm your soul needs.
So trust Him completely, let Him take control.
Rest in Him, allow Him to lead.

If you're wondering how I know He is there
I'll tell you, I just talked to Him.
He's listened, and answered, and been my life's joy.
I've walked mountains and valleys with Him.

As I met Him today and we talked about you
A sweet peace has come once again…
For He has things firmly within His control
So look up! Your hope is in Him!

He's listening, and caring, and loving you so
Precious friend, He's life without end!

When the phone rang today, I was so excited to hear the voice at the other end of the line say, "This is Lorraine. I've been free of cancer for some years now."

Praise and glory to God were the outcome of Lorraine's sufferings. Now as she shares her testimony of healing with others, they will realize that their "hope is in Him."

As you read Psalm 42: 8 and 11, praise God for His power to heal and His refuge of hope.

Psalm 42

8 Yet the LORD will command his loving kindness in the daytime, and in the night his song shall be with me, and my prayer unto the God of my life.

11 Why art thou cast down, O my soul? and why art thou disquieted within me? hope thou in God: for I shall yet praise him, who is the health of my countenance, and my God.

Craig's education was certainly an evidence of the Lord's sufficiency for our need. When we entered evangelism, we were concerned about providing the best possible education for Craig while traveling full-time. Several friends in evangelism recommended Calvert School, which offered an excellent accredited correspondence program for kindergarten through grade eight.

Craig was two years old when we began this music ministry, and at age five, he began his formal schooling. Morning hours were spent in study, and our travel trailer doubled as a classroom. Our travels enriched Craig's lessons, for we visited every historic place we could find. In addition, we toured factories, candy companies, clothing industries, record pressing plants, museums, and planetariums. Craig completed eight years of study through Calvert School with an "A" average in all subjects.

Then there was high school. We decided to use the independent study program of the University of Nebraska for his high school years. He maintained high grades in all of his classes, and decided to take the GED in order to get an earlier start on his career in art.

People often ask if teaching Craig was difficult. My reply is always the same. In a word, NO! The Lord has a way of equipping us for whatever confronts us, as we yield to Him. I look back now and smile when I think of how He planned it all. When I was in college, I thought I'd enjoy being a social worker, but my parents advised that I pursue a degree in education. I took their advice and was later able to use that education degree to teach my own son. The years of teaching him were precious to me, and I shudder to think what I would have missed if I had not been submissive to God's will.

As you read Proverbs 4: 5-13, praise God for the precious children He has placed in your care and thank Him for each opportunity He gives you to teach them His truth.

Proverbs 4

5 Get wisdom, get understanding: forget it not; neither decline from the words of my mouth.

6 Forsake her not, and she shall preserve thee: love her, and she shall keep thee.

7 Wisdom is the principal thing; therefore get wisdom: and with all thy getting get understanding.

8 Exalt her, and she shall promote thee: she shall bring thee to honor, when thou dost embrace her.

9 She shall give to thine head an ornament of grace: a crown of glory shall she deliver to thee.

10 Hear, O my son, and receive my sayings; and the years of thy life shall be many.

11 I have taught thee in the way of wisdom; I have led thee in right paths.

12 When thou goest, thy steps shall not be hindered; and when thou runnest, thou shalt not stumble.

13 Take fast hold of instruction; let her not go: keep her; for she is thy life

I grew up in a Christian home. It was my father who prayed with me when I trusted Jesus as my Savior. Although my father gave me many special things, I will always be most grateful that he cared enough to lead me to Jesus.

When our son, Craig, was seven years old, we shared a very precious moment together. As I was walking past the door of his room one night, he called to me in an anxious voice. His first words when I stepped inside his room were, "Momma, I want to be saved."

Ron and I had awaited this moment – the day when our son would trust Jesus – and now our family would be one in Him. We knelt by Craig's bed that night and prayed with him as Jesus became his Savior and Lord.

All parents want the best for their children. We may not be able to give them the material wealth of this world, but we can assure them of a heavenly treasure that can never be taken away. The material things of this world are only temporary. Jesus is forever!

As you read Matthew 6: 19-21, praise God for everlasting life through His Son. His most precious Gift is your eternal treasure!

Matthew 6

19 Lay not up for yourselves treasures upon earth, where moth and rust doth corrupt, and where thieves break through and steal:

20 But lay up for yourselves treasures in heaven, where neither moth nor rust doth corrupt, and where thieves do not break through nor steal:

21 For where your treasure is, there will your heart be also.

MEMORY 11

We had completed a revival at First Baptist Church in Dublin, GA on Wednesday night, and decided we'd drive home to Albany after the last service. The church was especially generous to our family, and we were so excited about all of the bills we'd pay with our week's salary.

There is no expressway between Dublin and Albany, so narrow country roads were unavoidable on our trip home. We were pulling our 29-foot travel trailer when the unexpected happened. We blew a tire on the travel trailer, and had no spare tire to replace the flat. We pulled off the road, and Ron unhooked the car from the trailer. It was with great apprehension that we left our "home on wheels" by the side of the road to head for the nearest town in search of a trailer tire. Needless to say, that was a difficult task at midnight. We found nothing, so we returned to our trailer by the side of the road and spent the night. The next morning, we found a gas station that had four tires, plus the spare we had needed for the two years we had driven on faith!

As we headed for Albany on our new tires, we thought about God's special care for us through the night. He had also provided for us financially before the need occurred. We actually had the answer before the question! What a joy to trust in a faithful Father.

As you read Psalm 28: 6-7, thank God for the many times He has answered your prayers and praise Him for the experiences which cause you to exercise your faith.

6 Blessed be the Lord, because he hath heard the voice of my supplications.

7 The Lord is my strength and my shield; my heart trusted in him, and I am helped: therefore my heart greatly rejoiceth; and with my song will I praise him.

MEMORY 12

What do you people do during the day? Do you sleep 'til noon and just work an hour at night? Do you have any friends? What do you really do for a living? Do you always smile?

These are questions we've answered throughout our ministry. I guess it isn't an "average" lifestyle, but being in the center of the Lord's will is the sweetest, most joyful life one can experience. I can honestly say that we don't tire of traveling, and the presence of Jesus in our hearts accounts for our smiles.

During revivals, our travel trailer was parked next to the church. We tried to be presentable by nine o'clock each morning. With three people and one small bathroom, that's saying a lot. Mornings began with prayer and devotionals. Craig and I started schoolwork between 8:30 and 9:00 AM while Ron began work in a temporary office at the church. He worked on publicity, scheduling, mail-outs, agendas for the evening service, etc. Sometime there were morning services, followed by lunch at the church. We also sang for numerous schools, nursing homes, civic clubs, prisons, hospitals, and senior citizen luncheons.

We would try to spend a few hours of family time each afternoon. Since evenings were filled with church activities, and mornings were occupied with school and morning services, the afternoons were an important time for us. We might visit points of interest or Ron and Craig might enjoy a game of basketball in the church gym, a trip to the comic book store (Craig had a huge comic book collection), or video games at the mall.

Craig made many friends in our travels, and sometimes they would skateboard, ride bikes, draw, swim, etc., depending on the area and the availability of concrete, paper, and water.

We thank God for allowing us to be together as a family in this music ministry. It's a sweet joy to walk with Him, to sing of Him, and to abide in Him.

As you read Joshua 24: 2 and 15, may you know the joy that comes from making Him Lord of your household. Determine this day that you and your house will serve Him.

Joshua 24

2 And Joshua said unto all the people …

15 … " choose you this day whom ye will serve … but as for me and my house, we will serve the Lord."

MEMORY 13

"Craig, you don't want to be fat like your mother, do you?" "Claudia, you remind me of my daughter-in-law. She's overweight, too." "I was trying to describe the Hendersons to my mother, and I said, 'It's the little man with the big wife.'"

It is sometimes difficult to smile and be gracious when hurtful remarks come our way. Hurtful remarks are one of Satan's tactics for defeating us... for making us feel worthless and unfit to serve.

For most of my first thirteen years in evangelism, I was overweight. The eating habits of evangelists and the lack of exercise in our daily schedules contribute to the problem. Many people took offense if we didn't eat a particular dish they had prepared, and sometimes pastors and churches disregarded our physical needs, scheduling three or four eating "fellowships" a day.

I finally decided to seek medical help for my weight problem. I found a Christian doctor who stressed the importance of bringing glory to God in one's physical appearance, as well as developing a beautiful spirit. The doctor set a weight loss goal of 90 pounds for me. With a diabetic diet and only 800 calories a day, I began my quest. I turned the matter of my weight over to God, knowing that His strength is made perfect in my weakness. He was able to do in me what I could not do in my own power. I lost 94 pounds, and I use the victory as a testimony to the faithfulness and power of the Great Physician.

As you read I Corinthians 6: 19-20, think about how precious you are to Him... and when you come to the realization that you are bought with a price, He will become even more precious to you.

I Corinthians 6

19 What? know ye not that your body is the temple of the Holy Ghost which is in you, which ye have of God, and ye are not your own?

20 For ye are bought with a price: therefore glorify God in your body, and in your spirit, which are God's

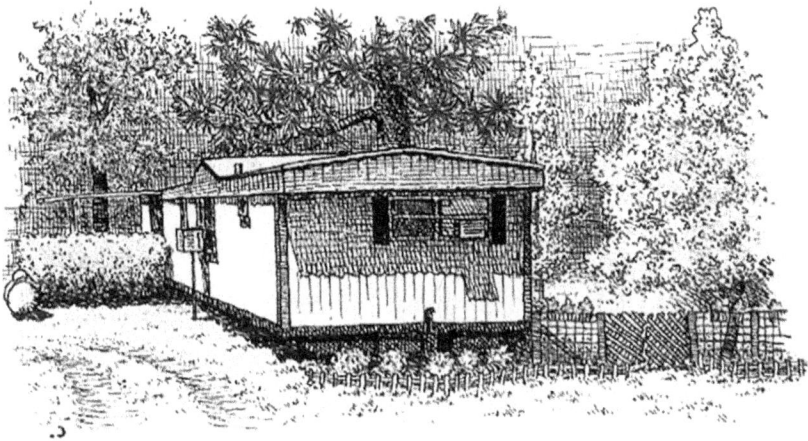

It is sometimes difficult to be content with the things that we have, especially when our material things are minimal by the world's standards.

Ron and I had been saving some money in hopes of making a down payment on a three-bedroom double-wide trailer. All of our married life we had lived in a single-wide, never owning any land. We kept looking at a beautiful mobile home with a large bedroom for Craig. His room was so small, and we were excited that the new place would be a special gift for him. We had worked out monthly payments, and it looked like the new home would be ours.

What we wanted, and what God wanted for us were two different things. There was an unexpected surgery, mounting bills, and little work scheduled. In a matter of months, our savings account was depleted, and we were in earnest with the Lord about our financial needs. We came to understand that we needed to be content with the shelter God had provided for our family and that in His timing something better would be ours.

We started cleaning out closets, getting rid of unused things, and we found that we had more room than we realized. New blinds in Craig's room, an uncluttered floor, and shelves for organization, made his "closet bedroom" into a comfortable retreat.

The whole experience was one of patience and submission, and our perspective changed. Our permanent address is "HEAVEN", and our home is an eternal one, designed by the Master Builder!

As you read John 14: 2-3, thank God for the assurance of your eternal home, through the nail-scarred hands of the Carpenter, His Son.

John 14

2 In my Father's house are many mansions: if it were not so, I would have told you. I go to prepare a place for you.

3 And if I go and prepare a place for you, I will come again, and receive you unto myself; that where I am, there ye may be also

MEMORY 15

Before entering evangelism, we thought evangelists were some of the "neediest " people we knew. Now that we are vocational evangelists, we still feel that way... but with a much greater understanding of the evangelists' financial situation.

Revivals and concerts are our primary means of support. There are many weeks when evangelists are unable to work. Sickness, weather, distance, no financial compensation, unexpected cancellations of scheduled engagements are all factors which effect finances.

Many people are under the impression that a revival love offering goes to the revival team. It has been our experience on numerous occasions to receive a small honorarium, when the love offering taken for the week totaled as much as $2000. We have also received a $300 honorarium for the week when the guest speaker (a local pastor with a regular income) was given the total love offering for the revival. Perhaps these situations are indications of why so many vocational evangelists are unable to survive for more than 18 months in this special calling. Again, it should be emphasized that God is our Sustainer and Provider, but sometimes man interferes, and God's work suffers.

As you read Malachi 3: 8 and 10, pray that God will be glorified in all that you do, say, think, or give. It all belongs to Him, and our use of His gifts should bring glory to His name

Malachi 3

8 Will a man rob God? Yet ye have robbed me. But ye say, Wherein have we robbed thee? In tithes and offerings.

10 Bring ye all the tithes into the storehouse, that there may be meat in mine house, and prove me now herewith, sayeth the LORD of hosts, if I will not open you the windows of heaven, and pour you out a blessing, that there shall not be room enough to receive it.

MEMORY 16

I've always been told I remind people of my mother. Our son, Craig, is a "carbon copy" of Ron. It's a great compliment to be told that we resemble someone we love.

In our ministry, Ron and I are often compared to other vocalists. Most people will say that we remind them of Roy Rogers and Dale Evans. That is a special compliment because of our high regard for Roy and Dale.

One of the sweetest compliments anyone ever pays us is to say that they see Jesus in our lives, or they hear Him speak through our music.

As I was thinking about family resemblances, I wrote this song, "Circle of Love", about my family.

Some think I sing like my mother.
    I look like my father, they say.
At times, I act like my brother;
    But I think he turned out okay.
What I'm really trying to say here
    Is easy to comprehend.
When God gave me this family,
    He gave me a circle of friends.

(Refrain)
They're so precious to me, my family.
My husband, our son, they're gifts from above.
They're so precious to me, my family.
God's special circle of love.

The purpose of every family
Should be to nurture its own,
With love, caring, and wisdom,
Where seeds of kindness are sown.
For the world is looking at our lives,
And we must point them to Him...
By living just like our Father,
Reflecting His love to all men.

(Refrain)
They're so precious to me, God's family.
We all become one through faith in His Son.
They're so precious to me, God's family.
His special circle of love.

As you read I John 4: 7-11, pray today that in all you do, the love of Jesus will be so prominent in your life that others will want to be a part of your spiritual family... "God's special circle of love."

I John 4

7 Beloved, let us love one another: for love is of God; and every one that loveth is born of God, and knoweth God.

8 He that loveth not knoweth not God; for God is love.

9 In this was manifested the love of God toward us, because that God sent his only begotten Son into the world, that we might live through him.

10 Herein is love, not that we loved God, but that he loved us, and sent his Son to be the propitiation for our sins.

11 Beloved, if God so loved us, we ought also to love one another.

People express love in a multitude of ways. Perhaps the most memorable expression of love to our ministry came during a revival in Mobile, Alabama.

When the offering was received, a diamond and ruby ring was placed in the offering plate. It was accompanied by a letter that read.

"Please accept my ring as a love offering to the revival team. They have touched my heart in a very special way. They may use it as they like. Whether they sell it and use the money, or whatever they choose, I pray it will be a blessing to them. I thank God for this beautiful church and the beautiful people in it. And I thank God for Jesus. No one could ever make a more precious sacrifice.
Love in Christ Jesus,"

This was such a special gift, and although we don't know the name of the giver, we know the name of the One for whom it was given!

As you read John 3: 16, thank Him for the greatest Gift... the Gift which gives meaning to all others.

John 3

16 For God so loved the world, that he gave his only begotten Son, that whosoever believeth in him should not perish, but have everlasting life

Seems like only yesterday that we packed everything into our little Ford Maverick and began a life of service "on the road". That was over 1,000,000 miles ago and 9 different vehicles. God has provided places of service in 19 states... over 400 revivals and over 1800 concerts. It has been a joy to see people come to Jesus in revivals, tent meetings, conferences, harvest days, concerts, homecomings, and special events.

Looking back, it's hard to believe we began this ministry with only a reel-to-reel tape recorder, a guitar, and a desire to share the love of Jesus through music. We knew God had a plan for our lives, and we were confident that He who began a good work in us would provide all that we needed to fulfill our calling.

We had only been in full-time evangelism for 5 months when we were invited to sing for the Georgia State Evangelism Conference in Augusta. We decided to sing "Say I Do" for the Conference. This was our first big statewide event, and we were scared to death. As we sang the chorus of the song (Anybody here want to live forever?, say "I do"), a pastor on the front row jumped up and shouted, "I Do"! Each time we sang that line, he led the congregation in shouting "I Do".

That pastor's enthusiasm was used of God to encourage our hearts and open doors of ministry through this experience. "Say, I Do" continues to be our most requested song!

As you read Deuteronomy 31: 8, be assured that God will be with you and give you courage to help you complete the work He has for you.

Deuteronomy 31

8 And the Lord, he it is that doth go before thee; he will be with thee, he will not fail thee, neither forsake thee: fear not, neither be dismayed.

MEMORY 19

Our schedule has often had its slack times. During the months of December and January, as well as June and July, booking engagements has always been difficult. The months of March, April, and May are usually quite busy. When one of our normally "busy" weeks was not scheduled for a revival or concert, we knew that the Lord had something else for us... and we looked forward to what He had planned.

Such was the case in May of 1988. We had a wonderful week of revival at Sugar Hill Baptist Church, and as the meeting concluded, everyone asked about our next engagement. We had tried to schedule revivals and concerts for the two weeks following the Sugar Hill revival – but nothing opened for us. We told the congregation at Sugar Hill that we were sure the Lord had something special planned. We just didn't know at that moment what He had in store.

We headed back to Albany on Thursday morning, and all along the way, I experienced severe back pain. This was strange, because I had never had back problems. The pain became so intense that at 1:00 AM on Friday morning, I found myself in the emergency room at Phoebe Putney Hospital. The problem was diagnosed as gall bladder... and on Saturday, I underwent gall bladder surgery.

Exactly two weeks after the Sugar Hill meeting, we had scheduled a concert. There were no engagements between Sugar Hill and the concert – so it wasn't necessary to cancel any engagements. The Lord blessed me with special strength that enabled me to sing just two weeks after surgery. It isn't always necessary to understand God's ways, but it is joy unspeakable to place your life in His care and trust Him for tomorrow.

As you read Psalm 118:14, thank Him for strength to stand in time of difficulty, and praise Him today with the song of love.

Psalm 118:19

14 The Lord is my strength and song, and is become my salvation

He has always been very special to me. I've known him since his birth in 1960. When he was a baby, I was his regular baby sitter. I watched him crawl, take his first steps, and listened proudly as he sang the songs he learned in Sunday school. He loved people, and was especially gifted at performing. He did magic shows, learned to play the guitar at age seven, and during his high school years, was the drum major for the school band. He had the lead role in many college musicals, and I was always so thrilled to hear him sing and see him perform. He had a dream of eventually working for the Walt Disney Corporation. In 1989, that dream became a reality when he was given a starring role in one of the Disney shows at Walt Disney World in Orlando.

His life has had a precious influence upon me. In everything he does, he has a zest for life, a smile, and an optimistic outlook. He never allows me to feel sorry for myself when things don't go right. When he experiences disappointments, he says, "There's always next time. I know the Lord has something better for me."

Thank you, Lord, for my brother, Claud. And thank you, Claud, for writing this "Simple Song of Love" for one of our albums.

A simple song, a song of love, that's all I have to give.

The only thing that I can offer is my life, the song I live.

No chorus lines, no flashing lights, just a simple melody

That sings of love found nowhere else...The love You've given me.

A simple song, a song of peace and hope for all who hear.

To know that You'll be by my side when no one else is near.

Through sunshine, the pouring rain, and to the rainbow's end,

Through everything this life may bring, I'll always have a Friend.

No "soap-box preaching," no begging, beseeching,

And I don't want to force them to see.

I just want to share, to tell people You care.

Please sing through me...

Your simple song, Your song of love; the song You came to sing.

To let us know You cared enough to give up everything.

So, help me as I live each day with people old and new

That through my life they'll hear Your song

And want to sing for You.

As you read Psalm 96:2, pray that others will hear His Song through the life you live.

Psalm 96:2

2 Sing unto the Lord, bless His name; shew forth His salvation from day to day.

The Lord has always been so gracious in meeting our needs. We never cease to be amazed by His timing... or His methods. In 1986, we presented a concert at a small church in Doerun, Georgia, under very difficult circumstances. As we were setting up our old Peavey sound system in preparation to sing, the system died! We tried everything possible to revive it, but all of our efforts failed. The church had a tiny "make-shift" amplifier into which we plugged our microphones, guitar, and tape recorder. We prayed "without ceasing" during the concert, and at the conclusion, we breathed a sigh of relief!

Now what? Again, we were totally dependent upon the Lord to provide a new sound system for our ministry. The system we had always wanted cost $2,000, but it was completely out of reach on our budget.

Just 3 days after the concert in Doerun, we found ourselves at a music store in Atlanta, check in hand for $2,000. We didn't have to borrow the money for a new system… nor did we charge it to Visa. The Lord spoke to someone about our need, and we were given "the desire of our hearts".

As you read Psalm 37:4-5, be assured that He will honor His promise as you commit your way unto Him!

Psalm 37:4-5

4 Delight thyself also in the Lord; and He shall give thee the desires of thine heart.

5 Commit thy way unto the Lord; trust also in Him; and He shall bring

There is a very special part of my life from which I have constantly drawn strength. I'm referring to the godly heritage I have in my grandmother and my mother. They instilled in me a love for home and family, and I've always desired to give my child the kind of love they gave to me.

My grandmother and mother were both creative people. They never sat down to watch TV without working busily at some craft... crocheting, knitting, etc. It's only natural when I think of them I recall the things they made with their hands. My grandmother's wedding rings were always prominent as she worked, and I admired those rings for many years. When she died, she left her diamond and ruby wedding rings to me. I wear them every day, and when I look down at my hands and see those rings, I'm reminded of the special love she had for me, the godly example she provided by giving of herself, and the heritage that I have because of her life. I too, must give my son what my grandmother and mother gave to me... so that he will know the love extended by the nail-scarred hands of Jesus.

As you read Matthew 7:24-25, remember that He is the greatest foundation upon which to build a heritage. Just as nails are necessary to hold a house together, so are the nail-scarred hands of Jesus necessary to build a heritage of faith.

Matthew 7:24-25

24 Therefore whosoever heareth these sayings of mine, and doeth them, I will liken him unto a wise man, which built his house upon a rock:

25 And the rain descended, and the floods came, and the winds blew, and beat upon that house; and it fell not: for it was founded upon a rock.

MEMORY 23

We were doing the music for a revival at a large church in the Atlanta area. We had scheduled many meetings back to back, so we decided to stay at the Stone Mountain Campground in our travel trailer during this revival, and enjoy the beautiful surroundings.

At about 8 AM, someone knocked on our trailer door. The church's Minister of Youth had come to deliver an urgent message concerning our family. As Ron opened the door, I heard the words, "Claudia's grandfather has died." The news was shocking and unexpected.

Death came for my grandfather the night before, as he was watching the World Series on television. He gasped for breath, lowered his head, and was gone.

My grandfather's sudden death made me realize how close each of us is to meeting Jesus. We're only "One Heartbeat Away" from the presence of our Lord. I wrote the following song from this experience and dedicated it to one who was ready to meet his Savior.

"One Heartbeat Away"

When He gave me life and health and time
And placed His song in my heart,
I thought I had tomorrow and forever.

But the years have passed so quickly.
Today is almost gone.
What will happen if He says,
"No more tomorrows."

I'll be just one heartbeat away for seeing Jesus.
I'll be one heartbeat away from the presence of the Lamb.
For those hands outstretched at Calvary,
Reached down in love and pardoned me;
And I'm just one heartbeat away from seeing Him.

He may call you in the hush of night,
The light of day, the pain of life,
and say, "I'm coming soon.
Your home is ready."

Will your heart rejoice to see His face;
To hear "Well done, you've claimed My grace?"
Or will you beg: "Lord, grant one more tomorrow?"

You're just one heartbeat away from seeing Jesus.
You're just one heartbeat away from the presence of the Lamb.
For those hands outstretched at Calvary
Reached down in love and set you free,
And you're just one heartbeat away from seeing Him.

As you read Matt. 24: 42 and 44, ask yourself if you are ready for His coming. Remember that you and I are only one heartbeat away for beholding the Lamb!

Matthew 24: 42 and 44

42 Watch therefore: for ye know not what hour your Lord doth come.

44 Therefore be ye also ready: for in such an hour as ye think not the Son of man cometh.

MEMORY 24

Having a dependable vehicle is a necessity in our line of work. With 265,000 miles on our 1978 van, we were truly traveling by faith. We priced a new cargo van ($17,000), but decided a new motor for our '78 van ($1,800) would be sufficient. The problem seemed simple enough, if we could raise $1,800. Actually, we had no problem. We had an opportunity to see God work.

As we were praying, the telephone rang... and we were invited to do the music for a revival at Milford Baptist in Marietta, GA. We had a wonderful week at Milford, and at the conclusion of the revival, Ron shared with the pastor (Bro. Jimmy Corbitt) our need for a new van motor. Ron told him that we had $500 for the motor, but we needed $1,300 more to cover the cost. Bro. Jimmy smiled, handed Ron our love offering and said, "Here's your motor!" The love offering was $1,363... and added to our $500, we had enough to purchase our "Milford" motor!

As you read Philippians 4:19, thank God for His faithfulness to provide for your every need.

Philippians 4:19

19 But my God shall supply all your need according to His riches in glory by Christ Jesus.

God's love is often overwhelming! Such was our experience when He provided us a house. We lived in our single-wide trailer for 23 years. Then one day as we were driving down a country road, we came upon an empty building (2,000 sq. feet) on 2 acres of land, and a sign on this property that read "For Sale". The building just happened to be a Kingdom Hall, but it had great possibilities for a home. In fact, the brown shingled, A-frame building looked like a house (although it had no windows!). Inside, there was one big open room with theater seats and a raised platform at one end. There were two restrooms consisting of three toilets and two sinks. No kitchen, no bathtub, and no room divisions! Perfect!

We bought this building, and between revivals and concerts, we worked on our house. For 18 months, we washed dishes in two 5-gallon buckets while we worked on the kitchen. Someone gave us the money to buy two windows for the dining room. Ron's sister gave us her old carpet for our bedroom. An uncle provided the light for our kitchen. It all came together to give us a lovely place to live.

Some people thought it strange that we would buy a Kingdom Hall and make it into a home. We just thought it was awesome that God would have the Kingdom Hall builders construct our house!

Revelation 11: 15

15 ... The kingdoms of this world are become the kingdoms of our Lord, and of his Christ; and he shall reign for ever and ever.

MEMORY 26

Has there ever been a time in your life when you knew God had kept you from harm? We were doing the music for a revival in the Savannah area in the Fall of 1994. The revival went through Friday, but we had to leave on Thursday, due to a prior commitment. The evangelist for the week was from South Carolina, and because his wife was unable to attend the revival, he planned to fly home and bring her back for the last two services of the meeting. A pilot in the church with a small private plane offered to fly him home, and we were invited to go along. We declined, and they flew to South Carolina without us. They picked up the evangelist's wife, unaware of the tragedy that was about to occur. Upon takeoff, the plane experienced a sudden downdraft, causing it to crash. The pilot survived, but the evangelist and his wife did not.

It was only by God's grace and divine intervention that we were not on the plane, because He had ordered our steps in another direction that day. As you read Proverbs 16:9, thank God for the many times He changed the course of your day by ordering your steps in a different direction to protect you from harm.

Proverbs 16:9

9 A man's heart deviseth his way: but the Lord directeth his steps.

MEMORY 27

I've never cared for the spotlight... and even after many years of music ministry, I still find it difficult to speak or sing for large groups of people. I have always loved the song, "No One Ever Cared For Me Like Jesus". I remember singing it before a mirror as a teenager, wishing for the courage to stand before people and proclaim the name of Jesus.

When I first began singing the song, I didn't really know the depth of the words. But as the years have passed, I've come to know just how precious the love of Jesus is.

I knew Him first as Savior when I was 10 years old. As the years passed, He became my Sustainer / Provider. There have been times during this ministry when Ron and I had no work and no money. (Our earned income for our first December in Evangelism totaled $50.) Only with the Lord's help could we have survived.

In 1972, the name Jesus meant Life-Giver. We were looking forward to the birth of our first (and only) baby. I entered the hospital on Sunday night, expecting an easy delivery. On Tuesday morning, 32 hours later, Craig was born... weighing 10lbs. 12oz. The hours between Sunday and Tuesday were critical, when both my life and Craig's life were uncertain. Prayer was crucial, and without the Life-Giver, there would have been no hope.

In 1983, the name Jesus meant Comforter. When I attended my grandmother's funeral, my heart was so grieved. But while I experienced grief, I was engulfed by an overwhelming peace, which subdued the sting of death.

In 1985, the name Jesus meant Healer, and I experienced His healing power first hand. After breaking my leg and being told by so many that it would never completely heal, the touch of the Great Physician's hand was sufficient for my need.

Today we often stand before large congregations and sing "No One Ever Cared For Me Like Jesus" and each time we sing those words, tears come to my eyes as I remember His love.

As you read Philippians 4:13 and 2 Corinthians 9:8, thank Him for being all that you need in all of life's situations. Because of Calvary, you too can say, "No One Ever Cared For Me Like Jesus."

Philippians 4:13

13 I can do all things through Christ which strengtheneth me.

2 Corinthians 9:8

8 God is able to make all grace abound to you, so that in all things, at all times, having all that you need, you will abound in every good work.

MEMORY 28

One of God's special blessings to our ministry has been the love and support of our pastor, Michael Catt, and our Sherwood church family. We joined Sherwood after moving to Albany in 1973. Our church has supported our ministry through prayer, encouraging words, financial gifts, and a multitude of unexpected blessings that have made a wonderful difference in our lives. Sherwood celebrated our 25th, 30th, and 40th anniversaries in Evangelism with beautiful receptions, monetary gifts, and even a letter of congratulations from Bill and Gloria Gaither! Sherwood has printed and mailed our ministry newsletter for many years. They were instrumental in the recording and premiere of two CD's ... "GRACE" and "Angel Band". They often help with expenses to the Southern Baptist Convention, enabling us to meet pastors, schedule concerts and revivals, and renew friendships with those in ministry. They have encouraged us and prayed with us through every obstacle we've faced.

We have had a precious friend in our pastor, and have appreciated his advice, direction, and encouragement through the years. He has always extended his hand to help meet our needs. His compassionate heart and the love of our Sherwood family are blessings that cause us to rejoice each time we remember God's sweet grace.

As you read Ephesians 2:8 and II Corinthians 12:9, thank God for His gift of saving grace, which He gave through His death on the cross, and His sustaining grace, which is sufficient for your every need! Give Him praise for the people He places in your life who extend that grace to you.

Ephesians 2:8

8 For by grace are ye saved through faith; and that not of yourselves: it is the gift of God:

II Corinthians 12:9

9 And He said unto me, My grace is sufficient for thee: for My strength is made perfect in weakness...

Do you know that "every good and perfect gift is from above"? All the precious blessings we receive come from the hand of our loving Lord. In fact, everything we have belongs to Him. When Ron and I began our lives as one, **we gave our marriage back to God.**

When He called us to this ministry, **we gave Him our voices**, and He has always been our Song.

When God gave us a precious son, we prayed over him, **and gave him back to God.**

When He provided a house for us, we prayed over our home, **and gave it back to God.**

With every vehicle we purchased, we prayed over it before we drove it off the sales lot (and often that prayer was with the salesman!), **and we gave each car or van back to God.**

So many wonderful gifts! But God's greatest gift to us was eternal life through faith in His Son, Jesus.

As you read James 1: 17 and Romans 6: 23, give thanks for God's goodness, and remember to praise Him for His greatest gift, eternal life.

James 1: 17

17 Every good gift and every perfect gift is from above, and cometh down from the Father of lights, with whom is no variableness, neither shadow of turning.

Romans 6: 23

23 For the wages of sin is death; but the gift of God is eternal life through Jesus Christ our Lord.

MEMORY 30

Looking back on our revivals and concerts, there were many memorable moments. Perhaps the revival at First Baptist Church, Garden City, GA in 1977 is one of our special memories. Ted Moody preached the meeting, and 51 professions of faith were recorded. The church had a youth ensemble that blessed our hearts that week and birthed lasting friendships with our family. The spirit of the church was joyful, and everyone was excited about such a great time of renewal.

God's presence has often been evident in the places we have served. He has always made a way where there seemed to be no way. During our early years of ministry, we were presenting a concert and using our reel to reel tape recorder for accompaniment. As we sang the last song of our concert, the tape recorder began a slow death. When the speed of the song became slower, the key we were singing in became lower. To keep the recorder going, Ron stuck his finger in the reel, trying to maintain the speed. We finished the song after singing it in several different keys! God saw us through a difficult circumstance and enabled us to complete the concert with confidence in the One who is able to do exceeding abundantly above all that we ask or think.

As you read Psalm 92: 4 and Psalm 34: 4, give thanks for God's presence, not only when you see the evidence of His mighty power, but also when you feel His provision in your time of need.

Psalm 92: 4

4 For thou, Lord, hast made me glad through thy work: I will triumph in the works of thy hands.

Psalm 34: 4

4 I sought the Lord, and He heard me, and delivered me from all my fears.

MEMORY 31

The prayers of family and friends have always been an essential part of our ministry. Although we don't know the names of everyone who has lifted us up, we are deeply grateful for the prayers and kindnesses in our behalf. Many people have extended God's grace to us in ways we never expected.

Our dear friends, Baker and Rebecca Thomas, not only pray for us, but in our early lean days in Evangelism, they helped us survive on fried bologna sandwiches. This provided a meal for us each week that we were not "on the road". Now that's a gift of grace with substance!

The love and prayers of our family have been much needed and appreciated. Ron's parents constantly pray for us, and their monetary gifts through the years, enabled us to get from place to place when churches didn't pay travel expenses.

God placed our ministry on the hearts of several people who continue to support us on a regular basis. We deeply appreciate their investment in our ministry.

One of our dedicated prayer warriors is my aunt, Beverly Davis. After seeing the "War Room" movie, she made a special prayer room in her home. The walls of the room are lined with names and prayer requests that she lifts up daily to the Lord. How we praise God for her and the many others who extend His grace to us through their prayers.

As you read Philippians 1: 3-6 and Romans 1: 9, give thanks for those people who pray for you without ceasing.

Philippians 1: 3-6

3 I thank my God upon every remembrance of you,

4 Always in every prayer of mine for you all making request with joy,

5 For your fellowship in the gospel from the first day until now;

6 Being confident of this very thing, that He which hath begun a good work in you will perform it until the day of Jesus Christ:

Romans 1: 9

9 For God is my witness, whom I serve with my spirit in the gospel of his Son, that without ceasing I make mention of you always in my prayers;

MEMORY 32

What do you do when your world suddenly collapses... when the days you face are filled with uncertainty, and the hope in your heart seems silenced by overwhelming circumstances?

On December 16, 2018, I awoke to find Ron on his knees by our bed, doubled over with excruciating chest pains. We assumed it was his heart, so we headed to the hospital emergency room. After a number of tests at the hospital, we were sent home. The following day at a routine visit with our family physician, Dr. Louise Wilder, she sent Ron back to the emergency room with a diagnosis of a serious gallbladder problem. The gangrenous gallbladder was then removed, but there were complications of a high white blood cell count and low kidney function. After the gallbladder surgery, Ron's urologist found a cancerous tumor on Ron's bladder. This required another surgery. When the tumor was removed, a stent was placed in the bladder to repair a hole left by the tumor removal. Surgery was also necessary on the prostate to restore normal function. Ron had 3 surgeries in 21 days. During this time of uncertainty, we prayed continually, living every moment with an assurance that God would make a way for our good and His glory.

As Ron continues the healing process, we rest in the outstretched arms of our Savior, praising Him for His healing power, amazing love, and unfailing promises. Our God is AWESOME, and His grace is truly sufficient for every need we have.

As you read Isaiah 43:2 and Hebrews 4:16 thank God for His all sufficient grace and a love that knows no limits. He is your Rock, your Redeemer, your Healer, your Provider, your Defender, your Friend, and may He always be your Song!

Isaiah 43:2

2 When thou passest through the waters, I will be with thee; and through the rivers, they shall not overflow thee: when thou walkest through the fire, thou shalt not be burned; neither shall the flame kindle upon thee.

Hebrews 4:16

16 Let us therefore come boldly unto the throne of grace, that we may obtain mercy, and find grace to help in time of need.

MINISTRY HIGHLIGHTS

Not only have the Hendersons enjoyed serving churches at the local level, but were honored with invitations to sing for the following state and national meetings as well:

· **GA State Evangelism Conference** (1976-Augusta), (1980-Macon), (1983-Savannah), (1986-Columbus), (1989-Jonesboro), (1994-Macon), (1997-Albany), (2006-Warner Robins)

· **GA State Pastor's Conference** (1979-Savannah), (1988-Macon)

· **SBC Evangelists' Conference** (1980-St. Louis), (1985-Dallas), (1987-St. Louis)

· **SBC Evangelists' Afterglow** (1992-Indianapolis)

· **GA Bapt. Convention - Sr. Adult Conference** (1992-Toccoa)

· **GA Bapt. Convention - Family Bible Conference** (1993-Toccoa)

· **GA State Directors of Missions Conference** (1997-Norman Park)

· **GA Bapt. Convention - Retired Minister's Meeting** (2000-Savannah), (2002-Atlanta)

· **SBC Evangelists' Retreat:** (2001-New Orleans)

· **SBC Sun. AM Worship Service - Sponsored by The Conference of Southern Baptist Evangelists:** (2001-New Orleans)

· **GA Bapt. Evangelists' Preaching Conference - Sponsored by The GA Bapt. Convention:** (2002-Jonesboro), (2003-Jonesboro)

· **GA Bapt. Convention - Sunday Night Rally:** (2007-Augusta)

. **AL Bapt. Convention - Pastor's Conference:** (2008-Montgomery)

. **Conference of GA Baptist Evangelists' Retreat** (2013 - Lithonia Springs)

. **GA Bapt. Convention - Pastor's Preaching Conference** (2014 - Macon)

. **SBC Evangelists' Southwest Sing-A-Long** (2019 Birmingham, AL)